Philip Jodidio

RENZO PIANO

1937

The Poetry of Flight

TASCHEN

Illustration page 2: Renzo Piano, 2002,
photograph by Gianni Berengo Gardin

Illustration page 3: Menil Collection, Houston,
Texas, USA, 1982–86

Illustration page 4: Centre Georges Pompidou,
Paris, France, 1971–77

© 2012 TASCHEN GmbH
Hohenzollernring 53, D–50672 Köln
www.taschen.com

Editor: Florian Kobler, Cologne
Design: Sense/Net, Andy Disl and
Birgit Eichwede, Cologne
Collaboration: Inga Hallsson, Cologne
Production: Tina Ciborowius, Cologne
Final artwork: Tanja da Silva, Cologne

ISBN 978-3-8365-3068-2
Printed in Germany

To stay informed about upcoming TASCHEN
titles, please request our magazine at
www.taschen.com/magazine or write to
TASCHEN America, 6671 Sunset Boulevard,
Suite 1508, Los Angeles, CA 90028 USA;
contact-us@taschen.com; Fax: +1 (323) 463-4442.
We will be happy to send you a free copy of
our magazine which is filled with information
about all of our books.

Contents

Introduction

Renzo Piano, 2000
Photograph by Michel Denancé

When Renzo Piano received the 1998 Pritzker Prize, the Jury Citation went a long way to explaining why this Italian-born architect is one of the most significant figures of his profession today. "The array of buildings by Renzo Piano is staggering in scope and comprehensive in the diversity of scale, material, and form. He is truly an architect whose sensibilities represent the widest range of this and earlier centuries—informed by the modern masters that preceded him, reaching back even to the 15th century of Brunelleschi—he has remained true to the concept that the architect must maintain command over the building process from design to built work. Valuing craftsmanship, not just of the hand, but also of the computer, Piano has great sensitivity for his materials, whether using glass, metal, masonry, or wood. Such concepts, values, and sensitivities are not surprising for someone whose father, uncles, and grandfather were all builders."

When Renzo Piano gave his acceptance speech for the Pritzker Prize at the White House, on June 17, 1998, he, too, made reference to his ancestors' profession: "I was born into a family of builders," he said, "and this has given me a special relationship with the art of 'doing.' I always loved going to building sites with my father and seeing things grow from nothing, created by the hand of man. For a child, a building site is magic: today you see a heap of sand and bricks, tomorrow a wall that stands on its own; at the end it has all become a tall, solid building where people can live." And he continued: "Architecture is an art. It uses technique to generate an emotion, and it does so with its own specific language, made up of space, proportions, light, and materials—for an architect, matter is like sound for a musician or words for a poet. There is one theme that is very important for me: lightness (and obviously not in reference only to the physical mass of objects). ... In my architecture, I try to use immaterial elements like transparency, lightness, and the vibration of the light. I believe that they are as much a part of the composition as the shapes and volumes." But where did this idea of lightness, indeed of flight, come from? Was it born of the careful study of architectural history, or did it have more to do with his upbringing?

City of Slate, City of Sails

To explain his thoughts, Piano inevitably refers to Genoa, where he was born. "Genoa," he says with a smile, "is a windy city where I played with the sheets my mother put out to dry and imagined they were sails on some great ship. Genoa is also a heavy city. Paul

Opposite page:
Centre Georges Pompidou, Paris, 1971–77
A crowd on the plaza and Montmartre in the background.

Centre Georges Pompidou, Paris, 1971–77
One of the most recognizable features of the Pompidou Center is its snaking escalator.

Valéry called it 'a city of slate,' but I grew up with the idea of doing the contrary."[1] Citing authors such as Italo Calvino, Renzo Piano makes the leap from these images of his childhood to a more adult vision of lightness. "When you begin to understand lightness," he says, "you discover that it is an attitude of the spirit. Intelligence can be heavy-going or light, and with age one discovers that a light intelligence is much more interesting."

Renzo Piano succeeds in being lighthearted even when it is clear that, for him, architecture is a deadly serious business. It is the balance that he strikes between weight and flight, between light and shadow, that sets him apart. Weight and shadow are part of any building, but Renzo Piano's architecture moves effortlessly toward the light. Bound by gravity and its own purpose, a Piano building nonetheless prepares to take flight at every instant. This is not a flight from responsibility; it is rather a lightness born of the understanding of weight.

Visitors must judge a building when they use it and often critics and architects themselves will speak of "style." Style might be equated with the personality of the creator of a work of architecture, and yet this is an idea firmly rejected by Piano. "Style is like a golden cage that you lock yourself into. Instead of giving myself joyously and freely to each new project, should I instead seek desperately to design a Piano building? One of the great beauties of architecture is that each time it is like life starting all over again. If you are only worried about being recognized you are making a huge mistake. You are being narcissistic and commercially minded. This is a negation of the very spirit of architecture. I don't like the word 'style,' but coherence is definitely something I seek."

Though he is very interested in art, Renzo Piano speaks more readily of artisans when he explains his work. The coherence or professionalism he seeks is bound closely to repeated gestures. "If I have to design a joint, why should I forget that I have done so a hundred times in the past? ... It is the repetition of gestures, like that of the artisan or the pianist, that creates what I call a 'stratification of experience.' What I seek is not

1 Author's interview with Renzo Piano, Paris, June 5, 2002. Unless indicated otherwise, all further quotations by Renzo Piano in this text come from this interview.

Centre Georges Pompidou, Paris, 1971–77
Many visitors to the Center come as much for the view as for the art.

style but a metabolism of experience." Piano's sympathy for the artisan's gesture may well have to do with his own background. His father, Carlo Piano, and his three brothers created the firm Fratelli Piano on the base of their own father's masonry business. They prospered after the war, building houses and factories as well as selling construction materials. Renzo Piano's older brother Ermanno, who studied engineering in Genoa, took over the business in 1965. Following his graduation from Milan Polytechnic Architecture School in 1964, Renzo Piano worked in the family company. Some of his early work, such as the Italian Industry Pavilion at Expo '70 in Osaka, was carried out in collaboration with his brother.

The Architect and the Engineer
After graduation, Piano entered a formative phase that included work in the offices of Louis Kahn in Philadelphia and the Polish engineer Zygmunt Stanislaw Makowski in London, a central figure in the development of space frames in contemporary architecture. Indeed, Renzo Piano has frequently underlined his admiration for engineers such as Pier Luigi Nervi, Jean Prouvé, and Buckminster Fuller, inventor of the geodesic dome, an admiration that has gone far beyond mere curiosity. His own working relationship with men like Peter Rice shows the enrichment he has brought to his architecture by delving deeply into the applied rigor of the engineer. Peter Rice (1935–92) worked on the Sydney Opera House (1960–67) before joining Piano & Rogers on the Pompidou Center project. "Peter," said Piano, "designed structures like a pianist who can play with his eyes shut." It is interesting that he refers both to his own work and to that of Rice by alluding to the art of the pianist. Yet there was no confusion about their respective roles. As Rice wrote: "The architect, like the artist, is motivated by personal considerations, whereas the engineer is essentially seeking to transform the problem into one where the essential properties of structure, material or some other impersonal element are being expressed. This distinction between creation and invention is

9

the key to understanding the difference between the engineer and the architect, and how they can both work on the same project but contribute in different ways."[2]

The architect's interest in details explains much of his relationship to the work of engineers, past and present. How does a building hold up, and what elegant, quietly innovative solution can resolve a given construction and design problem? These are the questions that Rice and others such as Tom Barker have answered with Renzo Piano throughout his career. Piano has said: "Knowing how to do things not just with the head, but with the hands as well: this might seem a programmatic and ideological goal. It is not. It is a way of safeguarding creative freedom."[3]

Technically oriented, Piano was also sensitive to the imaginative and optimistic point of view of figures like Peter Cook and Cedric Price (Archigram) whom he frequented when he taught for three years at the Architectural Association in London. If one imagines the work of Archigram, that of Louis Kahn, and also the soaring forms of Nervi or Fuller, one begins to imagine the sources of Renzo Piano's work. Nor is it surprising that he specifically rejected the siren call of postmodernism early in his career.

Learning the Art

Piano's earliest work, beginning in 1965, is often reminiscent of the technologically inspired work of other architects or engineers, although, significantly, he seems almost never to have consciously imitated another designer. Be it in his 1968 IPE Factory in Genoa with its reinforced polyester and steel roof, or his studies for a pavilion at the XIV Milan Triennial (1968), a continuous membrane design, Piano immediately challenged the conventions of architectural form. The Milan pavilion is remarkable because it represents a very early attempt to break out of the strictures of Euclidean geometry in architecture, seeking free forms related to elasticity and movement and in so doing anticipating some contemporary trends by more than 30 years.

Centre Georges Pompidou
Sculptures by Henri Laurens on the upper level of the Center.

2   Peter Rice, *An Engineer Imagines*, Artemis, London, 1994.
3   1998 Pritzker Prize brochure.

Centre Georges Pompidou
The IRCAM building to the left and the Stravinsky Fountain by Jean Tinguely and Niki de Saint Phalle.

It may be interesting to note that, although they did not know each other at the time, Renzo Piano and Peter Rice were already experimenting in related areas. Rice was working with the Structure 3 group at Ove Arup & Partners in London on a mixture of special cable and fabric structures, mostly with Frei Otto in Germany. Lightness is often associated with ephemeral structures, an idea that Renzo Piano espoused from the first. His 1966 Pomezia Factory was designed with polyester panels that could be dismounted to move the factory to another site, and his IBM Travelling Pavilion (1983–86) took these ideas to their logical culmination.

Piano's first international commission was the Italian Industry Pavilion for Expo '70 in Osaka. Built with his brother's firm, it was an exercise in lightness and rapidity. The reinforced polyester and steel structure was assembled in Japan in two months and drew considerable praise. The forms of this pavilion, though by no means as complex as those of the Pompidou Center, do bring to mind the later building. Its modular, suspended structure represented a voluntary juncture between industry and architecture, and Paris was soon to see the results of this experimentation on a much larger scale.

Expo '70 was indeed to have several important consequences for Renzo Piano. One of those who admired the Italian Industry Pavilion was the architect Richard Rogers. Even closer to the Pompidou Center in appearance and design, the administrative building for B&B (Novedrate, Como, 1971–73) was a first collaborative effort with Rogers. Again modular and suspended, the B&B structure also features the visible systems and bright blue, red, and yellow coloring that was to make a notable appearance in central Paris shortly thereafter.

A Factory for Culture
For both Renzo Piano, 35 years old, and Richard Rogers, 38, winning the competition for the Pompidou Center in Paris in 1971 brought almost instant international notoriety. After a number of small buildings, Piano was suddenly called on to design 100 000

11

Centre Georges Pompidou
The Brancusi Atelier seen from the third level of the Center.

square meters of space intended to showcase not only art, but also design, performing arts, and a library. The surprising shapes conceived by Piano and Rogers were to receive a mixed public reaction at the outset, but a steady flow of 20 000 visitors a day has marked the Center since its opening. "Beaubourg," says Piano, "was intended to be a joyful urban machine, a creature that might have come from a Jules Verne book, or an unlikely looking ship in dry dock ... Beaubourg is a double provocation: a challenge to academics, but also a parody of the technological imagery of our time. To see it as high-tech is a misunderstanding," he concludes.

Another significant participant in the Paris project was Peter Rice, who describes it in different terms: "It was a large, loose-fit frame where anything could happen. At its core was the belief, which had been identified in the brief, that culture should not be elitist, that culture should be like any other form of information: open to all in a friendly, classless environment."[4] Indeed, almost without knowing it, Renzo Piano, by winning the Pompidou competition, took a great step to defining not a style, but rather the coherence that he speaks of so convincingly today. Was the Pompidou Center a "parody of the technological imagery of our time," or was it aesthetically speaking a product of the 1960s, and therefore out of date from the first? With its flexibility and technical orientation, even in the details of its construction, the Center does bring together the fruits of industry and the general public in an edifice destined to break the elitist view

4 Peter Rice, *An Engineer Imagines*, Artemis, London, 1994.

Centre Georges Pompidou
The open platforms of the Center allow sculptures to be installed—and here provide a view of the Marais district of Paris.

of culture. The National Museum of Modern Art housed in the Palais de Tokyo, a new Center for Industrial Design (CCI), an experimental music facility (IRCAM) headed by Pierre Boulez, and a large library were also part of the brief.

Engineering, and indeed Peter Rice, also played a role in a second museum structure designed by Renzo Piano, the Menil Collection (Houston, Texas, 1982–86). In the period of nine years between the opening of the first structure and that of the second, Renzo Piano clearly moved toward a more mature approach to architecture. Still fascinated by details and materials, he no longer felt the need to display the technical "guts" of a building. As he says: "Paradoxically, the Menil Collection, with its great serenity, its calm, and its understatement, is far more 'modern,' scientifically speaking, than Beaubourg. The technological appearance of Beaubourg is parody. The technology used for the Menil Collection is even more advanced (in its structures, materials, systems of climate control), but it is not flaunted." Then, too, the project in Texas was very different in both scale and intentions. Rather than a state bureaucracy, the client—Dominique de Menil—in this instance was an individual. She insisted on the necessity of using as much natural light as possible and this led the architect to look at innovative systems for the control and utilization of the bright Texas sun.

Sometimes cited as Piano's best building, the Menil Collection is modest in appearance. Its walls are simple, and so, in appearance, is the roof. But Piano and Rice had carefully studied the ceiling and resolved the light problem with a modular leaflike system. Their solution called on unusual materials. As Rice wrote: "Ferro-cement and ductile iron were two of these materials. In combining them we sought to weave together the porcelain-like fragility of the ductile iron with the soft, grainy texture of the ferro-cement into a continuous melded whole."[5] With Menil, Piano's search for lightness and transparency reached new heights. He succeeded in subordinating the tech-

Menil Collection, Houston, Texas, 1982–86
Renzo Piano (standing) with the engineers Peter Rice and Tom Barker.

5   Peter Rice, *An Engineer Imagines*, Artemis, London, 1994.

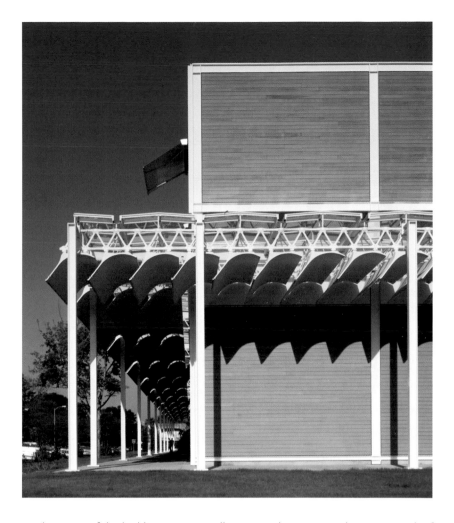

Menil Collection, Houston, Texas, 1982–86
The sunshades of the building were partially inspired by the forms of nature.

nical aspects of the building to its overall purpose, thus moving closer to a work of pure architecture, as opposed to an engineering *tour de force*.

The Transparent and the Opaque

In a way, Piano's goal came to be the consistent use of the best available technology in the least obtrusive way possible. What visitors noted most about his IBM Travelling Pavilion (1983–86), was not so much the building but what it displayed, and the views through its walls. Again, it was Peter Rice who worked behind the scenes to bring the architect's ideas to life. "The concept," explains Rice, "was to have a series of polycarbonate pyramids which, together with timber inner and outer members, would act as a semicircular arch spanning 12 meters and creating an internal space which would, when placed in a suitable natural setting, give the sense of being with nature." Designed to be moved from one location to another on specially designed trucks, the IBM Pavilion was both light and intentionally ephemeral. By adding transparency (coupled with appropriate sun shading) to the equation, Piano proved that far from being repetitive or superficial, contemporary architecture could invent new solutions to specific problems.

IBM Travelling Pavilion, 1983–86
Photographed here near the Castel Sant'Angelo in Rome.

In 1983, Renzo Piano took on a far heavier piece of architecture: the Lingotto automobile factory in Turin, praised by Le Corbusier in his 1923 manifesto *Vers une architecture*. Built between 1917 and 1920 by the engineer Giacomo Mattè Trucco, Lingotto was notable for its considerable size, and also for its rooftop car test track. Piano decided to keep its original form, while progressively adding new facilities. The first of these was a concert hall that he created by digging 14 meters into the inner courtyard (1990–94). The second was the heliport and Bubble panoramic meeting room (1992–95) that he perched on top of the structure. A more recent addition is the so-called Pinacoteca, designed to house the Agnelli art collection. Despite the apparent weight of the rooftop structure, it, too, seems poised to take off like the earlier helipad. When modernism was at its postwar height, dealing with as cumbersome a structure as Lingotto could only have inspired architects with a desire to raze it to the ground and start anew. Clearly sensitive to industrial heritage and personally interested in factory design, Renzo Piano brought an incremental approach to Lingotto, based on preserving its initial profile and linked to the desires of the client (Fiat), but his additions also ran counter to many modernist assumptions. When asked about the very heaviness of Lingotto, and the significance of his own interventions there, Piano replies: "It is a heavy building, but one that can still go forward. The Pinacoteca is symbolically and physically heavy ... Nonetheless it floats too, it flies above Lingotto. This is certainly not just a question of weight though, it is one of movement. One might speak of metamorphosis, of the capacity of something to transform itself."

The Call of the Pacific
Far from his native country, Piano took another major step toward the international recognition he has attained today when he won the prestigious competition for the Kansai International Airport Terminal (Osaka, Japan, 1990–94). Set on an artificial island located in the Bay of Osaka, the structure had to deal with the potential for earthquakes and the natural settling of the island. Although the land has dropped more than

Lingotto Automobile Factory, Turin, 1983–2003
The original test track on the roof of the factory was kept intact.

Lingotto Automobile Factory, Turin, 1983–2003
The Meridien Hotel was added to the complex in 2003.

experts predicted since the opening of the facility, the adjustable system of hydraulic pistons has proven equal to the challenge. Then too, set as close as Kobe to the epicenter of the so-called Hanshin Earthquake of 1995, Kansai Airport suffered no damage.

As is often the case, Renzo Piano describes his own buildings with a clarity that fully demonstrates the fundamental logic of his work. "With Tom Barker, a mechanical engineer with Ove Arup & Partners," he says, speaking about Kansai Airport, "we investigated streams of air, from which the form of the terminal's roof would emerge. In cross section, the roof is an irregular arch (in reality a series of arches of different radii), given this shape to channel air from the passenger side of the terminal to the runway side without the need for closed ducts. Baffles left open to view guide the airflow along the ceiling and reflect the light coming from above. We were creating an aerodynamic ceiling, concerned not with the flow of air outside, but inside. Kansai is a precision instrument, a child of mathematics and technology. It forms a strong and recognizable landmark; it has a clear and simple shape that declares itself without hesitation. It is a structure with undulating, asymmetrical lines. It spreads over the island like a glider—a missing link between ground and airplane. In the absence of other constraints, the only factor that has shaped its volumes is the space taken up by the aircraft and their maneuvering. The planes determine form, function, and extension. They are the true masters of the island. We have paid homage to these local divinities with a departure area that has 42 passenger-loading bridges and extends for 1700 meters, and is capable of handling 100 000 passengers a day. Kansai is one of the largest buildings ever built, three Lingottos in a row."[6]

If Renzo Piano's singular lack of "style" was not yet apparent in his production up to the early 1990s, his Jean-Marie Tjibaou Cultural Center (Nouméa, New Caledonia, 1993–98) made it abundantly clear. Here, he faced the challenge of building a cultural center dedicated to the Kanak civilization. He studied local culture before proposing a "village" made up of 10 spaces of different sizes and functions. For the most part approximately 28 meters in height, the structures face a main "street" on one side, and

6 1998 Pritzker Prize brochure.

expose their rounded wooden backs to sea winds. Making maximum use of natural ventilation, Piano ventured with the Tjibaou Center into the area of "sustainable" architecture. Much like "sustainable" development, this concept has many variants, but there is an implied respect for nature that Renzo Piano surely does not reject. As he said: "Nature is not made with the measure of man in mind. I personally love the sea, but despite 45 years of sailing, I still fear and respect it. If man didn't protect himself from nature, nature would see him off ... Man feels more comfortable constructing this new nature. It nevertheless happens that original nature is so powerful that only by interpreting it, only by using its own norms, can another be created."[7]

Renzo Piano's encounter with the Pacific, be it in Nouméa or in Japan, seems to have been significant in his development as an architect. He says: "I was 50 years old when I discovered the culture of the Pacific. It is a culture of lightness and of the ephemeral. Although I grew up in Europe, I feel much closer to the Pacific, where lightness, or the wind, is much more durable than stone. This is due to the ritual repetition of gestures from generation to generation. In Japan, there is no doubt that the culture of lightness and of the ephemeral is much more stable than the solidity of any stone. In California it is the tradition of Neutra and Eames, just as in Australia, architecture is often linked to the idea of the ephemeral."

Urban Man
In one of a series of large-scale urban projects he has undertaken since the mid 1990s, Renzo Piano has demonstrated his consciousness of the importance of scale and location. In 1996 he began work on one of the largest projects of his career, the reconstruction of a section of Potsdamer Platz (Berlin, Germany, 1992–2000). As he says: "Cities are beautiful because they are created slowly; they are made by time. A city is born from a tangle of monuments and infrastructures, culture and market, national history and everyday stories. It takes 500 years to create a city, and 50 to create a neighborhood. We have been asked to reconstruct a large chunk of Berlin in the space of five years." The most visible element of his contribution is the 45000-square-meter Debis Head-

7   Renzo Piano, *Sustainable Architecture*, Editorial Gustavo Gili, Barcelona, 1998.

Kansai International Airport Terminal, Osaka, Japan, 1990–94
An overall plan of the facility showing the main terminal and arrival gates near the top.

quarters, with its 21-story tower clad in a double skin of glass, obviating the need for excessive air conditioning or heating.

On a much smaller scale, Renzo Piano recently completed the Maison Hermès in Tokyo (1998–2001). This surprising glass-block structure is located in the heart of Ginza, one of the most vibrant and active commercial areas of the Japanese capital. As Piano says: "Architecture is capable of metamorphosis when it is based on the play and vibration of light. The Maison Hermès is a building that is made of nothing, and yet it changes 1000 times a day. The idea of lightness or flight is too simple to describe this. It is about the marvelous tension that exists between durability and the transient. The ephemeral is beauty in its purest state." Piano is of course being modest when he says the Maison Hermès is "made of nothing." The glass-block design required special manufacturing by Vetroarredo in Florence to meet stringent Japanese fire and earthquake standards. Whatever the weather conditions, the building shimmers in daylight and glows from within at night, becoming the "magic lantern" referred to by the architect.

Halfway around the world from Tokyo, Renzo Piano also made a substantial mark in Manhattan. Few really well-known international architects ever get the opportunity to build in New York, and Piano was selected for two projects. The 52-story New York Times Building is intended to be as open and transparent as possible, symbolizing the relationship of the newspaper to the city. Talking about the building Piano says: "I like fighting gravity. Magic is essential in architecture. Working in Manhattan, I love the idea that we accept the clear and simple geometry of a building. We accept that logic. But complexity comes from texture, from vibration, from the metamorphic capacity of the building to transform, to change, to breathe ... The building is actually very simple. But the complexity comes from the skin, the surface of the building actually vibrating, working with the weather."[8] Piano's second major project in Manhattan is equally prestigious if somewhat less visible—the Morgan Library on Madison Avenue—where, significantly, the better part of his design is located underground. In this case, he insists neither on the concepts of lightness nor of the ephemeral, though the glass-covered

8   Renzo Piano, interview by Robert Ivy, *Architectural Record*, October 2001, http://archrecord.construction.com/people/interviews/archives/0110piano.asp

area is anything but heavy. "There are buildings like the Morgan Library that are meant to last—and why not?—for a thousand years. That is how we worked. Why dig deep into the bedrock of New York? To safeguard the rare books of the Morgan ... forever."

Berlin, Tokyo, and New York are not the only major cities where Renzo Piano has worked recently or has new projects underway. In Sydney, within view of Jørn Utzon's Opera House, he completed the Aurora Place towers in 2000, and in London he has taken on a far more controversial effort to rise to the skies. His 305-meter-tall London Bridge Tower will be Europe's tallest office building. His own statement sets out his vision for this structure. "I see the tower like a vertical little town for about 10000 people to work in and enjoy and for hundreds of thousands more to commute to and from. This is why we have included shops, museums, offices, restaurants, and residential spaces within its 66 floors. The shape of the tower is generous at the bottom without arrogantly touching the ground, and narrow at the top, disappearing in the air like a 16th-century pinnacle or the mast top of a very tall ship ... Architecture is about telling stories and expressing visions, and memory is part of it. Our memory is permeated by history. That is why this design alludes to spires."

Roots in the Earth, Head in the Stars
One wonders how Renzo Piano retains his warmth and courtesy in the midst of his world-girdling list of projects. One wonders, too, how he approaches new work without ceding to the kind of repetitive "style" that he obviously rejects. "Things have changed a lot for me," he admits. "I used to be quite bad at 'listening' to sites. When you are young, your system of registering things is not yet fully formed. And I had such a joy in manipulating materials ... With age, we begin to understand some things better, don't we? I never get involved in a project without having spent some time on the site ... listening. I spend a day or two doing small sketches on the site. They are like a form of shorthand for me; I use them in order to be able to discuss certain points with my staff ... Forget about style, there is professionalism. We usually define the basic outlines of

Jean-Marie Tjibaou Cultural Center, Nouméa, New Caledonia, 1993–98
Inspired by local hut design, the structures rise to a maximum height of 28 meters.

a project quickly at the office, but afterwards there is a great deal of thinking and refining that is done. Architecture is slow work. Having a good idea at the outset is one thing. Keeping it right up to the end is another," he concludes.

Renzo Piano is an optimist, but a lucid one. How often does he balance one quest with its opposite, juxtaposing a form deeply rooted in the earth with the metaphor of flight, at Kansai Airport for example. It is also Piano's deep respect for the mechanics of architecture, and for the talents of great engineers that permits him to give something more to his architecture than an attractive façade. This is a man who lives and breathes architecture. Yet this is also a man who designs his own sailboats and leaves his office and work far behind every year to be on the sea. Technology can certainly be cold, but in Piano's hands, working with men like Peter Rice, it is bent to a will. Materials ranging from glass blocks to ceramic panels or Puglia sandstone in the case of the Padre Pio church are fashioned not as though they came off an assembly line, but rather as though the hand of the architect had individually touched them. An optimist, a modern humanist, a man smitten with love for his art, for his profession—these are all descriptions that fit Renzo Piano. In a profession where each element can weigh tons, Renzo Piano has succeeded in retaining the lightness of his youth, an enthusiasm and an openness that has the world beating a path to his door. Rather than a style, his clients have sought an approach that varies in accordance with each site, each function. Renzo Piano is a master of the mechanics of lightness. He knows that architecture is bound to the earth, but it is in the equilibrium of tension between earth and sky that he has found his place. The 250-ton Pinacoteca hovers on the roof of Lingotto, ready to take to the air. The wind fills the sails of Piano's boat *Kirribilli* and there, finally, movement is his.

1971–1977 ▶ Centre Georges Pompidou

Paris, France

The main façade with its snakelike escalators.

Inside the glass-clad escalators that rise to the top of the building.

Below:
A section drawing shows the large scale of the structure as compared to neighboring buildings.

The Georges Pompidou Center is in many ways a seminal structure, not only in the career of Renzo Piano, but also for the architecture of its time. "We were young and it was very much an 'in your face' kind of building," said Piano 20 years later. He may have almost regretted the overtly industrial appearance of the building that has tended to obscure its actual functions. Intended as a showcase of modern French culture in the spirit of President Pompidou, who also facilitated the growth of such urban experiments as the "Front de Seine," the Paris facility was a kind of a giant offspring of Malraux's "maison de la culture" concept. From the first, it embraced various disciplines and forms of expression, ranging from a library to the National Museum of Modern Art. Significantly, the engineer Jean Prouvé was a member of the jury that selected the young team of Renzo Piano and Richard Rogers. Prouvé's own Maison du Peuple in Clichy (1939) has been cited as a precursor of the concept of spatial flexibility so important to the Pompidou project. It was in a way the fulfillment of many 20th-century technological fantasies like those of Buckminster Fuller, but here, with the brilliant assistance of the engineers Peter Rice and Tom Barker, the dream took very real form. Six stories high, with a 48-meter clear span, the Center stands out near the old Marais district of Paris as an ode to technically oriented architecture, with its web of tubular ducts on the east façade and the signature glass escalator, inching up the 166-meter-wide west face. Piano's office sums things up in another way. They say that "Beaubourg," as the Center is more commonly known, was "a double provocation: a challenge to academics but also a parody of the technological imagery of our time." The Pompidou Center, they conclude, "is a 'celibate machine' in which the flaunting of brightly colored metal and tubing serves an urban, symbolic, and expressive function,

An aerial view confirms the factorylike impression given by the architecture.

Opposite page top:
The Forum space opening on the main entry level of the Center.

Opposite page bottom:
At night, the Center glows from within, revealing the activity that continues every day until closing time.

not a technical one." The original Center included the underground facilities of the IRCAM, a contemporary music complex headed by Pierre Boulez. In 1988–90, Piano added a new, above-ground structure for the IRCAM, just across the street from the Pompidou Center. Its composite brick façade clearly announces that by that time the architect had set aside the Archigram style complexity that characterized the main building. Another small addition to the Center, the Brancusi Atelier, was added in the early 1990s. Brancusi left numerous sculptures to the French government on the condition that they remain in his atelier. The officials of the Center and Piano approached this condition with a unique combination of modern architecture and a faithful reconstruction of the original studio on the plateau in front of Beaubourg. Coming back to the Pompidou Center to oversee its renovation in the late 1990s, Piano cleared the structure of the overly fussy additions brought to the interiors by other designers and gave it back a good measure of the transparency and openness with which it had been designed. Significantly, it could also be said that his renovation calmed the discordant assemblage of mechanical forms that had characterized the galleries and other interior public spaces from 1977 on.

1982–1986 ▸ **Menil Collection**

Houston, Texas, USA

A sketch by Piano shows the scale of visitors vis-à-vis the gallery height and the screens.

Below:
The basic form of the structure is purely geometric, but the sunscreen and the light columns give it an airy openness.

It was in 1981 that Dominique de Menil approached Renzo Piano about building a museum for her family's collections of Surrealist and African art in Houston. The design of this structure, calling on natural lighting to the greatest extent possible, seems to be at a great distance from the visibly technological complexity of the Pompidou Center. Conceived 10 years after the Paris building, it is visibly a work of maturity. Working once again with the engineers from Ove Arup & Partners, Piano carefully studied the incidence of light within the exhibition galleries, particularly important in this part of the United States where harsh sun is the rule. It was Dominique de Menil who insisted that the works be visible in the best natural lighting conditions obtainable. The ground-floor exhibitions are complemented by a rooftop "Treasure House" open on appointment and designed in a denser, storage-oriented mode for some 10 000 works of art. The system of ferro-cement and cast ductile iron "leaves" devised for the control of interior lighting extends beyond the walls of the museum to cover pedestrian passageways running alongside. The history of the Menil family's collecting and commitment to modern art is edifying. Having begun to collect art under the influence of Marie-Alain Couturier, the Dominican friar who was largely responsible for Le Corbusier's work at La Tourette and Ronchamp, they also came to appreciate architecture. Their Houston home was built by Philip Johnson in 1948–49, and they organized the first one-man museum show of the work of Max Ernst in the United States in 1952. Beginning in 1964, they worked on the famous Rothko Chapel. Designed by Philip Johnson, it was dedicated in 1971. Renzo Piano succeeded in giving built form to their

Generous ceiling height and ample natural
light allow works to be seen well.

Above:
The final version of the ground floor plan with
opaque galleries in the lower part, and brighter
ones in the upper section.

family tradition of openness and deep interest in the arts and architecture with his
design. Dignified and calm, fitting in well with the environment of small wooden houses, the Menil Collection is one of the first real masterpieces of Renzo Piano's career.
Piano added a second structure to the Menil Collection. The Cy Twombly Annex (1992–
95) is located across Branard Street from the original structure. A square grid with
eight rooms, one of which has a double volume, is formed with concrete block walls
and a light roof designed to bring ample daylight into the exhibition areas. Piano
describes this form as a "butterfly alighting on a firm surface."

Opposite page top:
The collection offers a surprising contrast
between primitive art and modern pieces.

Opposite page bottom:
African art is seen against the backdrop of an
enclosed garden.

1985–2001 ▶ **Redevelopment of the Old Harbor of Genoa**

Genoa, Italy

Inspired by harbor cranes, Piano's elevator is seen in his sketch.

Opposite page:
Both sails and cranes evoke the atmosphere of the port of Genoa.

Below:
A broader view of the harbor installation by Renzo Piano.

The city of Genoa decided late in the 1980s to organize an international exhibition to commemorate the 500th anniversary of the discovery of America by Christopher Columbus. The site selected for the event was part of the old port of Genoa (wharves dating from the 17th to the 20th century), which permitted both the renovation of a historic area of the city and the construction of new, permanent facilities. The project was also to create a new link between Genoa's historic center (near the port) and the sea. In practical terms, the project entailed restoring the old buildings along the port, such as the three-story, 400-meter-long Cotton Warehouse, to provide various facilities, including a library and auditorium. Great care was taken to ensure that these renovations did not betray the original spirit of the district. New buildings, such as an aquarium and a naval derrick—a crane symbolizing the new port—were built, with an equal attention harmonizing with the spirit of the port. Extending the area's short streets to the waterfront created the port's link to the city: Via del Mare, one of the main thoroughfares of the historic district, was extended along a breakwater near the aquarium, leading to the center of the port. More than the execution of a construction or renovation plan, the project was intended to reclaim something of the port's glorious past. That wager seems to have been won since this part of the city has taken on a life of its own, both night and day.

1983–2003 ▶ Lingotto Factory Conversion

Turin, Italy

The rehabilitation of the Lingotto Factory, a symbol of industrial Turin, is a project that Renzo Piano has been working on since the early 1980s. Built between 1917 and 1920 by the engineer Giacomo Mattè Trucco, Lingotto was praised by Le Corbusier in his 1923 manifesto, *Vers une architecture*. From the first, Renzo Piano decided with the client Fiat to retain the fundamental characteristics of the original building. Further, it was decided that the renovation would be a phased project, with each new addition being completed whether or not other elements were ready. Technology of various types was considered the leitmotif of the Lingotto renovation. As Piano wrote: "Once completed, the Lingotto will be a genuine machine, capable of interacting with the climate and linking up to all the communication systems in existence."

Between 1992 and 1995, Renzo Piano added the Heliport and Bubble Panoramic Meeting room to the former factory. With a capacity of 24 people, the Bubble offers an extensive view of Turin. With its cantilevered helicopter landing pad and the Bubble's own futuristic double-skinned glass dome, this addition was a clear sign that Lingotto was being brought into the present. For Piano it was also a characteristic movement from the earthbound solidity of the original factory to a lighter mode. The Bubble appears to float above Lingotto, and the attached helipad reinforces the idea of architecture taking flight. Between 1990 and 1994, a Concert Hall was added to the old factory. Built by digging 14 meters below grade into an inner courtyard, this music facility was designed in collaboration with Arups and with Helmut Müller for the acoustics. The

Opposite page top:
Piano dubbed this addition for the Agnelli art collection the "flying bank vault."

Opposite page bottom:
The exhibition gallery is perched on top of the old factory structure.

structural work on the heliport, Bubble, and concert hall was finally carried out by Fiat Engineering. More recently (2002), Renzo Piano added the Giovanni and Marella Agnelli Art Gallery to Lingotto. As his grandson Lapo Elkann said, speaking of Giovanni Agnelli on the occasion of the opening: "He never concealed his ambition: to shift the center of gravity in Turin in this direction, transforming a former factory into a new center, a new magnet for the future development of this city. This development also opens up new dimensions: services, commerce, specialized university education, culture, tourism, and leisure. Conceived on a grand scale and superbly designed over 80 years ago, the Lingotto possessed great potential for change. Naturally it needed careful renovation to adapt it to its new functions and needs. Thanks in part to the contribution and collaboration of local public institutions, this process of transformation took 11 years to be completed. Once again, the Lingotto is full of life and activity." As early as 1961, Agnelli had asked the architect Carlo Scarpa to design a museum at Villar Perosa, but Scarpa died in 1978 and that project was never carried out. Speaking himself of this project, Giovanni Agnelli says: "Those who come to visit Lingotto will see an area of the outskirts of Turin—between the Alps and the hill on which the city stands—that I have always loved. One of Renzo Piano's special gifts as an architect is that his designs seem to inject new life into the area around a new building, a new project; the entire place becomes a sort of resonance chamber for the building under construction. The houses, the urban fabric, the metropolis itself become a sort of network, at the center of which the traveler finds a moment of aesthetic repose and reflection." The Pinacoteca, like the Bubble, appears to hover above Lingotto near the edge of its famous test track, its flat roof and ship-like body seemingly poised to fly higher still.

1990–1994 ► Kansai International Airport Terminal

Osaka, Japan

A section drawing shows the curving roof and different levels of the terminal building.

Opposite page:
An aerial view of the main terminal.

Below left:
Inside the spacious passenger area of the terminal.

Below right:
The long, low curvature of the building is visible in this image.

One of the largest architectural and engineering undertakings of the late 20th century, Kansai International Airport was built on a 511-hectare artificial island located in the Bay of Osaka. Piano was selected from a prestigious field in an international competition in 1988. The unusual curved shape of the 1.7-kilometer-long main terminal building is related to air traffic control's need to maintain visual contact with taxiing aircraft at all times. Piano used this formal constraint to the benefit of his design, making reference to works of art such as Brancusi's *Bird in Space*, and aircraft or gliders. It will not escape visitors that the undulating roof also recalls wings for this island airport. The curve of the terminal was, in fact, conceived as a small section of an imaginary 32.8-kilometer-diameter torus, whose main volume would be underground. With its 83-meter-long arches on the upper floor, the terminal offers a real feeling of freedom to travelers. It should be noted that the construction of such a large building on an artificial island posed many technical problems, solved in good part with the assistance of Ove Arup & Partners and Nikken Sekkei, using a system of hydraulic joints designed to compensate for the predicted settling of the landfill. Although its visible structure may under some angles recall the design of the Pompidou Center, Kansai Airport has a flowing ease in its design that was certainly born of Piano's experience. Simply put, the traveler finds his way easily in this airport and, even more important, feels comfortable at all times. Seen from the air, the 82 000 stainless-steel panels covering the 90 000-square-meter roof often shine in the sun, offering a more congenial image than almost any other modern airport in the world. The scale of Kansai International Airport is such that it coincidentally gave rise to a series of other projects, such as Tadao Ando's Awaji-Yumebutai complex built on the nearby island of Awaji on the site deeply scarred by the extraction of landfill for the airport.

1989–1991 ▶ Renzo Piano Building Workshop

Punta Nave (Genoa), Italy

The roof of the structure seems to flow directly into the sea.

Top right:
A sketch by Piano shows the stepped design and its exposure to the sun.

Opposite page:
Viewed from above, the building is to the right in this image.

Initially linked to a study carried out with UNESCO on "Mediterranean natural structures," the Renzo Piano Building Workshop (RPBW) offices are laid out in an unusual configuration, on a slope to the west of Genoa, facing the sea. The stepped design recalls neighboring terraces that cascade down toward the shore. An eight-person funicular serves the facility. Conceived like a greenhouse because of the need to study plant species, the structure is designed with a laminated wood frame roof set on thin metal columns. Double glazing with an intermediary layer of air helps to keep heat gain as low as possible, while admitting a maximum amount of natural light to the work areas and offering views to toward the sea. Exterior mounted slat shades reduce the penetration of direct sunlight into the workspaces. Aside from the stone and earth wall on the mountainside, the other walls of the structure are also made of glass. According to Renzo Piano, this atelier is made of "space, sun, and nature." Despite his frequent use of technological means, the architect carries his passion for lightness over into the conception of simple and elegant designs such as that of this structure. Making no attempt to carve into the hillside, he prefers to adapt architecture to its site, and to make the interior fully permeable to natural surroundings. In this type of work, Renzo Piano is closer to so-called green architects than he is to any "high-tech" designer.

Renzo Piano at his desk in the Punta Nave offices.

Below:
An overall plan of the Punta Nave building.

Opposite page top:
A section drawing shows the interior spaces and the continuous roof.

Opposite page bottom:
The interior is entirely open to its natural setting.

41

1991–2001 ▶ **Banca Popolare di Lodi**

Lodi, Italy

In this project, for one of the largest banks in the Lombardy region of Italy, Renzo Piano proposed an approachable, friendly design, conducive to vegetation and open to pedestrian traffic. The client wished in any case to avoid the fortresslike structures of so many banks. In terms of the overall design, Piano has chosen to make use of cylindrical structures of varying height clad in terra-cotta whose forms and colors evoke a nearby medieval castle and the silos of farmsteads frequently seen in the region. Set on the site of a former dairy farm in the midst of an industrial zone where the Polenghi Lombardo factory was located, the bank is nonetheless at the intersection of two of Lodi's major arteries, close to the train station and the downtown area. Various openings punctuate the large succession of rectangular blocks on the west façade, giving access to a large square inside, covered by a light glass-and-steel cable structure that serves as the meeting place for pedestrians. It is this square that leads to the bank's offices and to an 800-seat auditorium. Retail outlets and other offices have also opened in the complex and the constant movement of pedestrians makes the bank a center for the life of the community.

The plan above shows the entire facility, with the round auditorium in the center.

Right:
The interior of the auditorium.

Opposite page:
Exterior view with the radiating "spider web" pattern of the canopy.

1993–1998 ▶ Jean-Marie Tjibaou Cultural Center

Nouméa, New Caledonia

Opposite page:
traditional hut being built near the Center.

Below:
The independence leader Jean-Marie Tjibaou for whom the Center was named.

Below right:
Though he uses wood for interiors, Piano still creates modern, light spaces.

Few architects have built in such far-flung locations as Renzo Piano. Even by his standards though, New Caledonia in Melanesia is a bit off the beaten track. Subsequent to the significant difficulties encountered with the population of New Caledonia by the French government in the late 1980s, it was decided to build a Kanak Cultural Center near the capital of Nouméa. Taking his clue from the disposition of local villages, Piano conceived this center, set on a narrow peninsula, as a series of wooden pavilions. On the side facing a lagoon with strong dominant winds, the architect erected a series of curving wooden-walled structures ranging from nine to 28 meters in height. While a double-skinned design makes these façades sufficiently resistant even during tropical storms, they are also designed to admit natural light and breeze while encouraging the expulsion of hotter air through a natural "chimney" effect. There are three functional "villages" in the complex. The first contains the public areas and exhibition spaces, the second the auditorium, médiathèque, and meeting rooms, and the third the administrative and teaching areas. Despite his logical emphasis on local culture, Renzo Piano

45

An aerial view of the complex, which sits alone on a green peninsula.

Below:
An overall plan of the complex.

here blends the use of wood and natural ventilation with glass and aluminum elements. A visit to the Center is conceived as a stroll through the carefully preserved tropical environment. One quality that sets Renzo Piano apart from other talented architects is his ability to adapt his designs to their locations while maintaining a constant interest in materials and appropriate technology. Even when using metaphors, Piano varies his approach. Where the roof of Kansai Airport can be said to resemble a wing, the pavilions of the Jean-Marie Tjibaou Center are as much like sails as they are reminiscent of local hut design. His subtle references are never so literal as to become obvious. A master of modern, abstract architecture, he nonetheless succeeds in adapting his architecture to the most varied sites and functions.

1992–2000 ► **Potsdamer Platz Reconstruction**

Berlin, Germany

Seen from the exterior, the buildings are typically light and modern—Piano's contribution to Berlin's reconstruction.

Top:
An elevation drawing shows the different elements of the complex.

Opposite page:
Inside the Theater and Casino building.

The reconstruction of Berlin's Potsdamer Platz was one of the most ambitious urban development programs of the late 20th century. Destroyed during World War II and the later construction of the Wall, plans for reconstruction of the square began in 1990 with the organization of a competition for the site south of the Tiergarten, east of Scharoun's Preussischer Staatsbibliothek and west of Leipziger Platz. A master plan by Hilmer & Sattler was chosen and individual landowners began to select architects. Daimler Benz picked Renzo Piano for their master plan and for the construction projects on five of the 15 planned sites. Piano determined the general configuration of the streets and buildings and stipulated that all of the structures should have copper roofs, and use clear glass and materials resembling terra-cotta for façades. RPBW worked here in association with Christoph Kohlbecker. Other architects involved in these projects included Rafael Moneo, Arata Isozaki, Richard Rogers, and Hans Kollhoff. The first completed project by Piano was the Debis Headquarters, a 45000-square-meter building made to look like four structures rather than one. Although it contains a monumental 28-meter-high atrium, one of the most remarkable features of the Debis Headquarters is the double-skin glass façade design for the east, south, and west elevations of the 21-story-high tower. A layer of pivoting glass panels is set 70 centimeters outside the inner glass wall. Opened by a system of sensors during warm weather, the double skin obviates the need for excessive air conditioning. Terra-cotta screens are used on the outer layer of the lower sections of the complex. An Imax Theater designed by the Renzo Piano Building Workshop faces the rear of the Debis block, reinforcing the urban continuity established by the architect, despite the insistence of one architect to use other materials for the façades of the neighboring Hyatt Hotel. The Convertible Imax Theater, also known under the name B7, is a 15600-square-meter mixed-use building including the theater, a restaurant, and retail spaces. The 440-seat theater is located in a sphere 36 meters in diameter that is integrated into the building. The spherical volume of the theater rises above the building and is visible from a distance. The sphere is also visible from the street through a 1000-square-meter clear glass façade.

1991–1997 ▶ **Beyeler Foundation**

Riehen (Basel), Switzerland

The walkway leading to the main entrance.

Below:
An elevation drawing shows the long, low form of the building.

Opposite page:
Transparent spaces allow visitors to view sculptures by Alberto Giacometti from outside.

Built on a site close to the German border in the Basel suburb of Riehen, the Beyeler Foundation is an exercise in architectural restraint and mastery. The long, narrow site also includes a park area and connects to a former house serving as a shop, café, and museum offices. Located next to a busy road leading toward the Black Forest, the building is designed with a Patagonian porphyry wall closing off the street side. This stone is also used for other museum areas. Within the galleries, white walls and light wood floors give a degree of the serenity requested by the Foundation's founder, the art dealer Ernst Beyeler. This calm seems to be almost the direct antithesis of the busy "high-tech" approach of the Pompidou Center. An emphasis on natural lighting gives optimal viewing conditions for the impressive collection of impressionist and modern art accumulated by Beyeler, as well as the numerous works shown during temporary exhibitions. It can be noted that the Beyeler Foundation was completed the same year as the much-vaunted Bilbao Guggenheim by Frank Gehry. It would be difficult for two museum structures to be so different. Where it comes to showing fine works of art in an environment that places them in their best light in every sense of the word, there can be no doubt that the Beyeler Foundation is a far better instrument than Gehry's sculptural fantasy. Rather than seeking to express his own artistic ambitions, Renzo Piano has wisely chosen to reflect the wishes of his client and to honor the artworks the Beyeler Foundation contains. Though he may have garnered fewer articles in the press, Renzo Piano's achievement here is more in tune with the times than the explosively heroic approach seen in Bilbao.

1997–2001 ▶ Niccolò Paganini Auditorium

Parma, Italy

Seen from the exterior, the structure looks like an almost empty shell.

Below:
A sketch by Piano showing the main auditorium at the center.

Opposite page:
A night view of the building with its internal structure fully visible.

The Paganini Auditorium was built inside the former Eridania sugar factory, a heterogeneous group of industrial buildings. Set near the historical center of Parma, the area is now a park, known for its tree and shrub specimens. Despite its original function, the main building was well proportioned from an acoustical point of view, and Piano took the unusual liberty of eliminating the transversal walls, replacing them with three large glass façades. A system of soundproof panels hung from the trusses over the stage participates in the spatial organization of the main area. Even though the building is 90 meters long, the use of glazing permits it to be transparent from the outside and allows guests not to lose sight of the park. Leading to the entrance, a row of double lanterns frames the approach path. The public enters through the south end of the building, and proceeds through the building's length. A first high-roofed, open-air space leads inside, passing through a wide glass wall. From this point, visitors continue on to the two-level foyer. Located at the north end, the 250-square-meter stage offers enough space for large musical ensembles, including a choir and orchestra. In a most unusual configuration, the rear of this stage is nothing other than a glass wall, giving an almost unimpeded view of the park beyond. The 780 seats are set on a slightly sloping surface covering an area of 590 square meters, ensuring good visibility from all seats. Other former factory units were used for the service and rehearsal spaces.

1998–2001 ▶ Maison Hermès

Tokyo, Japan

It may be significant that Renzo Piano's projects outside of his native Italy are rarely isolated cases. Well after the completion of the Kansai International Airport terminal, he remains a highly respected figure in Japan, and it is not surprising that the French fashion house Hermès called on him for their flagship store located in the Ginza area of Tokyo. The most striking feature of the 44.55-meter-high structure is its façade made of 13 000 45 x 45-centimeter glass blocks. Made by Vetroarredo in Florence, with supports manufactured in Switzerland and installed in Japan, the glass blocks are a successful example of international collaboration in contemporary architecture. The glass blocks were specially manufactured to meet stringent Japanese fire and earthquake standards. Each block is intended to be able to move as much as four millimeters, absorbing any potential seismic shock. Conceived of as a "magic lantern" particularly because of its luminous nighttime appearance, the structure may recall such modern icons as Pierre Chareau's Maison de Verre, but it also retains a distinctly Japanese flavor. The filtered views of the outside world seen from within are images from a floating, liquid world. There is a lightness in this glass wall that brings to mind the best of Japan's traditional architecture. On a 580-square-meter site, the architect has built a 6071-square-meter building, with some 1150 square meters used for actual sales areas. The building also includes a large space for temporary exhibitions and a small "museum" of the history of the house of Hermès (designed by Hilton McConnico). There are 10 stories above ground, and three below. As fashion houses call more and more on well-known international architects for their boutiques in Tokyo, particularly in the Ginza and Omotesando areas, Renzo Piano's Maison Hermès will stand out as an exceptional blend of European modernity and Japanese perception.

A section drawing exposes the narrow floor design.

Opposite page:
The transparent glass block building stands out in this night view of Ginza.

1994–2002 ▶ Parco della Musica Auditorium

Rome, Italy

An aerial view of the entire complex.

Top:
An overall plan shows the forms of the Parco della Musica from an angle similar to the aerial photo.

Opposite page:
The closed, shell-like lead cladding of the buildings.

In what is undoubtedly his largest project in Italy, and his first in Rome, Renzo Piano set out to create "a city dedicated to music." Located in the Quartiere Olimpico created for the 1960 Summer Olympics, on the main road leading into Rome from the north, the complex proved its adaptability early in the construction process when the ruins of a fourth-century farmhouse villa were discovered on the site. This discovery held up work for a year and had to be integrated as a museum into the final design. Piano rotated the entire design and moved it six meters to the north to accommodate this discovery. The complex is made up of three lead-covered auditoriums respectively seating 2800, 1200, and 750 people, and each facing a 3000-seat outdoor amphitheater. The first of these, the largest of its kind in Europe, is designed for symphonic concerts, and like the smaller ones boasts a good deal of flexibility, for example in stage configurations. The 1200-seat hall is meant for ballets and contemporary music, while the smallest facility will be used for operas, baroque music, and theater. Although the City Council of Rome originally asked Piano for a 3000-seat indoor auditorium, analysis of acoustics determined that no more than 2800 could actually hear music properly without amplification. The acoustics of the facility were worked out by Helmut Müller in collaboration with Pierre Boulez and Luciano Berio. Another incident in the early phases of the project concerned the wood paneling chosen by Piano for the auditorium interiors. Italian laws do not establish any regulations regarding the use of layered wood mixed with steel in public works; the Supreme Council for Public Works would have had to approve it and would, therefore, have preferred standard materials to be used. But in the end, Piano managed to impose his choice of American cherry panels. Piano has stated that he had Hans Scharoun's Berlin Philharmonic and Library in mind in designing the Roman structures. Opened officially by Walter Veltroni, the mayor of Rome, on April 21, 2002 (though not yet fully completed at that time), the complex is surrounded by three hectares of park area newly planted with 400 trees.

The 1200-seat concert hall is essentially rectangular with a rounded exterior shell.

A section drawing shows how the roof envelops the concert space.

An interior view of the 2800-seat concert hall.

Right:
A section drawing showing the same space,
with its curved roof.

1996–2000 ▶ **Aurora Place**

Sydney, Australia

Aurora Place is a mixed-use project situated near Sydney's Royal Botanical Gardens. Two towers, an 18-story residential building, and a 41-story office structure, make up the complex. A light glazed canopy links the two blocks and announces the openness of the design at ground level. A degree of warmth is achieved by the use of glazed terracotta tile cladding where glass panels are not used. Both towers have subtly curved and folded façades that might echo the sail-like forms of Jørn Utzon's nearby Sydney Opera House. Piano's personal interest in sailboats comes to mind here too. Typically, Piano has innovated in the outer shell, using glass panels whose opacity can be varied by changing the size and position of the frit. A good deal of attention is paid to the comfort of users, for example with the winter gardens on the office floors that have operable glass louvers to allow air to come in. In the apartment building, each apartment cuts through the entire floor, giving bedrooms a view toward a plaza, and living rooms overlooking the Royal Botanical Gardens. Although the office tower is imposing, with its 49000 square meters of floor space and 200-meter height, the complex remains approachable and "human" in good part because of Piano's close attention to detail and to aspects such as ventilation and sun shading. Set against the background of Sydney's numerous high-rise buildings, Aurora Place fulfills Piano's stated ambition in this case, to make a tower that is "not just a pile of unrelated office slabs, but a real vertical piece of the city."

An elevation drawing shows the configuration of Aurora Place vis-à-vis neighboring buildings.

Below right:
A transparent glass façade opens toward the Royal Botanical Gardens.

Opposite page:
Piano's building stands out in this view from the Gardens.

1999–2003 ► **Nasher Sculpture Center**

Dallas, Texas, USA

As is often the case in the United States, the Nasher Sculpture Center was created at the behest of a wealthy individual, Raymond Nasher. The entire $60-million cost was borne by his foundation. Though a Bostonian, Nasher has long lived in Dallas and made his fortune with shopping centers. An avid collector of modern sculptures, he decided to buy a plot of land adjacent to the Dallas Museum of Art to exhibit his works. Originally a parking lot, the 150-meter by 60-meter site includes a 4000-square-meter gallery for the more fragile works. The building consists of six travertine marble walls, defining five bays. The three center spaces, covered by a curved glass roof, contain the exhibition spaces, while the other bays and the basement house a bookshop, cafeteria, auditorium, offices, gift shop, and the Nasher Institute for Modern Sculpture. The outdoor exhibition areas are four to five meters below grade, so that the works look as though they had come from an archeological dig. Since it opened in October 2003, it has attracted at least 200 000 visitors. Raymond Nasher was inspired to choose Renzo Piano as his architect in large part because of his admiration for Piano's Menil Collection building, but the two men met at the opening of the Beyeler Foundation in Basel. Nasher, a client of Ernst Beyeler's, bought works by Rodin, Miró, Tinguely, Matisse, and Giacometti from the Swiss dealer.

1999–2005 ▶ **Zentrum Paul Klee**

Bern, Switzerland

The site of the Zentrum Paul Klee is outside Bern, close to the artist's tomb, in a landscape of gently rolling hills, with the Alps in the distance. It was this topography that inspired the design of the museum itself, although the site has been considerably altered due to nearby roads, including a highway leading out of Bern. Intended to house 40 percent of the 10 000 known works of the Swiss artist, the structure is integrated into three artificial hills. The first of these hills contains a 300-seat auditorium and a museum for children. The middle hill contains the main exhibition space, with space for temporary shows below ground. The final volume contains works not on public display and a center for the study of Klee's oeuvre. Due to the sensitivity to light of many of the artist's works, overhead natural light is not really part of this scheme, and part of the roof is covered with vegetation, emphasizing the symbiosis of the architecture with the landscape. That said, Piano pierced the roof at various points to bring in daylight, where the conservation of the works permits. The arches forming the volumes of the complex are clearly inspired by naval construction. As Piano says, the shape of a boat is not dictated by any real concerns of geometry, but rather by the rules of movement through water.

Seen from the rear against the backdrop of
fields, the building blends into the landscape.

Left:
A model shows how the arches of the building
dip below grade.

Opposite page top:
Galleries offer some natural light but must
also protect the fragile works.

Opposite page bottom:
Interior spaces maintain the rhythm of the
exterior of the building.

1999–2005 ▶ High Museum of Art Expansion

Atlanta, Georgia, USA

It was subsequent to the 1962 crash of a plane carrying Atlanta's arts community leaders that Robert Woodruff of the Coca-Cola Company created the Woodruff Foundation. Today, the Woodruff Arts Center includes the Alliance Theater Company, the High Museum of Art, the Atlanta College of Art, the 14th Street Playhouse, and the Atlanta Symphony Orchestra. The original High Museum was designed by Richard Meier, and opened to the public in 1983. With its central atrium inspired by Frank Lloyd Wright's Guggenheim, the Museum includes about 5000 square meters of exhibition space for works which can be viewed from many different angles through the space of the building, and a 200-seat auditorium. Since its completion, the High has nearly doubled the size of its collection and has 500 000 visitors per year. These facts led the Woodruff Arts Center to ask Renzo Piano to add 16 000 square meters of extra facilities, including additional gallery space, enlarged special exhibition areas, and improved visitor amenities. Piano designed three new buildings: a main pavilion, a special collections building, and an administrative office structure. A glass bridge links the main pavilion, with its "expansive, light-filled lobby," to the Meier building at the ground level and the top floor. Piano's plans include other elements of the Woodruff Arts Center campus to create a "pedestrian-friendly village for the arts." As Piano has stated: "In planning the design of the High and the Woodruff Arts Center, we had the challenge of serving the needs of this established museum of fine art, while integrating its design with that of the entire Woodruff Arts Center campus. We set out to create a vision for the entire campus—a dynamic center for art and culture—that would invigorate the people and the cultural life of the city." The total construction budget stood at $163.4 million. Additionally, a $15-million endowment goal had been set, bringing the budget for the entire project to $178.4 million.

The building's ribs allow light to penetrate while giving an impression of solid forms.

Opposite page:
Piano's signature lightness is visible in this plaza view of the expansion.

2000–2006 ▶ Morgan Library Renovation and Expansion

New York, New York, USA

A section drawing showing the auditorium below grade.

Opposite page:
Top, the main entrance on Madison Avenue.
Bottom, the interior piazza.

Below right:
The new auditorium also seen in section above.

Serving as both a museum and a library, the Morgan Library is home to one of the world's largest and finest collections of rare Medieval and Renaissance literary and musical manuscripts, books, prints, and drawings. Created by the financier J. P. Morgan (1837–1913), the Library was housed in a building designed by New York architects McKim, Mead & White in 1903. The Morgan Library later extended to the Morgan Library Annex Building, built in 1928, and subsequently to a series of other extensions, including the former mansion of the Morgan family (1853). With the goals of rendering this situation more rational and of increasing visitor and storage space, the Library called on RPBW. The architects expanded the Morgan by a third without exceeding the height of the historic structures through digging into the bedrock beneath the Library. A 299-seat auditorium, a three-level storage vault, and mechanical spaces were thus housed below grade in new space. Above ground a new glazed "piazza" creates a sense of unity and coherence between the old and new areas. A new public entrance on Madison Avenue was created, and the existing buildings significantly renovated. A 6-meter cube was added at ground level for displaying masterpieces and as an element uniting the earlier McKim and Annex buildings. A new four-story building directly connected to the Morgan Mansion was added on the north side for offices that face the piazza and 37th Street. The Annex Building was made into the main gallery space, and a new bookshop, café, and small restaurant were also added.

2000–2007 ▶ The New York Times Building

New York, New York, USA

A sketch by Piano with concentric circles around the newsroom.

Below right:
The building carries the famous logo of the daily newspaper.

Opposite page:
The structure stands out from its setting near Times Square.

According to Renzo Piano: "The New York Times Building, at 8th Avenue and Times Square, has a very strong urban presence. The building is designed to be part of the street on which it stands. On the ground floor, there is a garden and an auditorium. In a way this approach may be more European than American." Chosen over Norman Foster, Frank Gehry, and Cesar Pelli, Piano's design for the 52-story building is intended to be as open and transparent as possible, symbolizing the relationship of the newspaper to the city. The façades employ a combination of clear glass curtain walls and a scrim of white ceramic tubes hanging 61 centimeters outside the glass. Acting as a sunscreen, the tubes obviate the need for tinted or fritted glass. Underway in 2000, and reconfirmed after the attacks on the World Trade Center, the New York Times Building is seen as a sign of confidence and commitment to the city. The newspaper occupies the lower half of the structure while a real-estate development firm, Forest City Ratner, is commercializing the rest of the space. The six-story base of the tower includes an atrium for shops and restaurants and an auditorium for lectures. A roof garden is protected by extensions of the glass curtain wall above the actual building height. *The New York Times* has had several locations in Manhattan, including its Tower on 42nd Street opened on January 1, 1905, and its most recent structure, on West 43rd Street, modified three times since its 1913 completion. Because of its considerable height, central location, and vocation, the New York Times Building is one of the most prestigious commissions to be given to a foreign architect in recent years in Manhattan.

2005–2008 ▶ California Academy of Sciences Renovation and Expansion

San Francisco, California, USA

The green roof of the building is one of its most remarkable features.

Below right:
Seen from a distance, the Academy seems to blend into its green setting.

Opposite page:
A light canopy shelters a walkway in a typical gesture by Renzo Piano.

This large project was completed in late 2007, but the work of installing the museum went on into 2008. The project had a total budget, including exhibition facilities, of $370 million. Founded in 1853, the California Academy of Sciences is housed in 12 buildings, built without a master plan over a period of 80 years, beginning in 1916. It is the only combined Aquarium, Planetarium, and Natural History Museum in the United States and is located in Golden Gate Park. It was in 1989, when some of the facilities were damaged in the Loma Prieta earthquake, that the Academy began its plans to upgrade the facilities. Piano's plan includes a "village-like cluster of spaces under a contoured roof." The environmentally friendly roof, measuring about 1.5 hectares, is covered with vegetation, making the new building "almost a piece of the park," according to the architect. A partially glass-enclosed piazza forms the central space of the completed project. Renzo Piano worked with the local architects Gordon Chong & Partners on this project, in which only one of the existing buildings, the Neoclassical beaux-arts Africa Hall, was restored. Other historic features of the Academy, such as the barrel-vaulted ceiling of the Steinhart Aquarium and the North American hall, are, however, evoked in the new complex. The whole "incorporates environmentally responsible construction technology and recycled and renewable building materials into an aesthetically accomplished master plan." Large windows offer views toward the park, but Piano's design actually reduced the "footprint" of the complex by making more

Vegetation is also present within the domed spaces lit by circular skylights.

Below:
Like the "Bolla" on the Lingotto Factory, a spherical form animates the interior volume.

The entrance to the expansion where a bridge provides access to the warm interior.

Below:
A section drawing showing the relation of the green roof to the internal spaces.

efficient use of interior space and employing underground construction. As opposed to completely distinct areas, the Academy "features flexible, integrated exhibition spaces that reflect the interconnections of the living world and the multidisciplinary nature of science."

Modern Wing of the Art Institute of Chicago

Chicago, Illinois, USA

sketch by Piano showing the simple form with the projecting roof of the new Wing.

Below:
Transparency is skillfully combined with the protective nature required of art exhibition buildings.

Opposite page:
Both light and airy, the modernity of Piano is fully visible in this image.

The city of Chicago has embarked on a large-scale cultural program centered on the Lakefront Millennium Park, a 10-hectare former zone of railway tracks and parking lots. Frank Gehry has designed a 200-meter-long trellis and a band shell for the park, while Renzo Piano has been called on to build a $200-million addition to the Art Institute of Chicago. His L-shaped building is replacing the former Goodman Theater at the corner of Columbus and Monroe. Using glass, steel, and limestone, Piano has carefully thought out the connection between the old and the new—the old being the original 19th-century beaux-arts museum buildings. A "minimalist" pedestrian bridge across Monroe Street will connect the park to the cultural facility. The 25000-square-meter addition will have what has been called a "flying carpet" roof. Though this design is seen locally as being a complement to Gehry's pavilion in the park, this airy form of roof is also seen in the Pinacoteca recently added to the Lingotto factory in Turin. With the development of the Lakefront Park, the Art Institute of Chicago, one of America's richest museums, will be located between two green areas, since it is also close to Grant Park. An essential element of the program was that the new structure links the two older existing buildings, straddling a railway line. Piano refers to immense railroad tracks as being the starting point of his inspiration for this structure. In an interesting homage to a great Chicago architect, Renzo Piano has proposed to relocate the entrance arch of Louis Sullivan's demolished Chicago Stock Exchange Building (formerly at the southwest corner of Monroe and Columbus) closer to the museum's preserved and renovated "Stock Exchange Trading Room."

This gallery view shows the Chicago skyline
with Frank Gehry's band shell in the exterior
foreground.

A section drawing shows the relation of the
interior of the Wing with the bridge that
extends into the Park.

The new building seen from beneath the bridge
that leads to Millennium Park.

2001–2010 ▶ Central Saint Giles Mixed-Use Development

London, UK

A sketch by Renzo Piano shows the brightly colored blocks that make up the complex.

Below right:
A drawing showing the final version of the scheme.

Opposite page:
A photo showing the angled and articulated links between the blocks.

The Central Saint Giles Mixed-Use Development in London includes 56 apartments, 53 "affordable" flats, 37000 square meters of office space, and a public piazza with a restaurant and retail spaces, on a 7000-square-meter site. The residential tower was acquired and completed by United House Developments. The buildings are marked by their colorful façades, made up of 134000 green, orange, lime, and yellow glazed terracotta tiles. Renzo Piano states: "The color idea came from observing the sudden surprise given by brilliant colors in that part of the city. Cities should not be boring or repetitive. One of the reasons cities are so beautiful and a great idea is that they are full of surprises, the idea of color represents a joyful surprise." The buildings are grounded around a courtyard in the center of the site, open to the exterior by pedestrian paths. The project received an award for the Best Commercial Workspace from the British Council for Offices (BCO, 2011). The complex was completed in May 2010, and is located near the east end of Oxford Street where an office building erected in the 1950s was formerly occupied by the Ministry of Defence. The new complex includes a 15-story west block with the 109 residential units, and the larger 11-story eastern block for offices featuring the largest floor plates of any office building in West London. Though originally somewhat controversial, the colorful complex has attracted such prestigious office clients as NBC Universal and Google.

Right:

A plan shows the higher residential block to the left and the larger U-shaped office element to the right.

Below, an aerial view with the residential building to the bottom of the image.

An interior view with full-height glazing
offering a generous urban view.

Right:
A glass block sitting above the ceramic-clad
main façade.

Left:
A drawing shows the ceramic cladding system
in the scale of the building.

85

2001–2010 ▶ Los Angeles County Museum (BCAM and the Resnick Pavilion)

Los Angeles, California, USA

An elevation drawing of the Broad Contemporary Art Museum (BCAM).

Below:
The exterior escalator of the BCAM.

Opposite page:
The travertine clad façade of the BCAM with its signature red elements.

The Los Angeles County Museum of Art (LACMA) is situated on an eight-hectare plot of land including 10 buildings. Renzo Piano was the project architect for the program (with Gensler acting as Executive Architect) called "Transformation" which included the Broad Contemporary Art Museum (BCAM, 2008) and the Lynda and Stewart Resnick Exhibition Pavilion, completed in 2010. The BCAM has 5574 square meters of gallery space, and the BP Grand Entrance, which is a 750-square-meter open-air pavilion and orientation space. The roof of this pavilion includes solar panels intended to power a work by Chris Burden called *Urban Light*. Located north of the BCAM, the Resnick Pavilion is a 4180-square-meter structure. Clad in Italian travertine, the BCAM features a red "spider" escalator on its north façade. The Resnick Pavilion, built at a cost of $53 million on top of a parking garage, has an open-floor plan with concrete floors and a saw-tooth roof with vertical glazing. LACMA bills the Pavilion as "the largest purpose-built, naturally lit open-plan museum space in the world." The eastern and western walls of the Resnick Pavilion are clad in pale travertine marble that comes from the same quarry as the marble used for the BCAM's façade. To the north and south, Renzo Piano has used glass cladding. The mechanical systems and exterior technical

A 2006 sketch by Piano shows the relative
position of the BCAM and the Resnick Pavilion.

Below:
The open-plan exhibition space in the Resnick
Pavilion.

rooms of the Pavilion are colored in the same "Renzo Red" used for the BCAM escalator. Piano said of the overall LACMA master plan: "If you are designing a museum you offer contemplation. It is not enough for the light to be perfect. You also need calm, serenity, and even a voluptuous quality linked to contemplation of the work of art. Achieving such a result at the Los Angeles County Museum of Art depends on integrating the new museum into its broader context. That is the purpose of a master plan."

Below:
The external mechanical elements of the Resnick Pavilion, colored "Renzo Red."

Below right:
The BCAM (left) and the Resnick Pavilion (center) seen in an aerial view of the LACMA campus.

2004–2012 ▶ London Bridge Tower

London, UK

In March 2002, Southwark Borough Council gave permission to build a £350-million 66-story tower above the London Bridge tube station. The 305-meter-tall structure will be Europe's tallest office building. With nearly 90 000 square meters of space, it will contain offices, hotels, restaurants, and apartments. Dubbed the "Spike" or "shard of glass," the building has elicited considerable controversy but won over the support of London's then mayor, Ken Livingstone. Though economic conditions and events such as the September 11 attack in New York may give some second thoughts about the construction of such visible towers, Renzo Piano strongly defends the idea. His own statement, made in November 2000, makes it clear why. "This is my vision," he says, "I see the tower like a vertical little town for about 10 000 people to work in and enjoy and for hundreds of thousands more to commute to and from. This is why we have included shops, museums, offices, restaurants, and residential spaces within its 66 floors. The shape of the tower is generous at the bottom without arrogantly touching the ground, and narrow at the top, disappearing in the air like a 16th-century pinnacle or the mast top of a very tall ship ... Symbols," he continues, "are dangerous. Often tall buildings are aggressive and arrogant symbols of power and ego, selfish and hermetic. I don't even think we should strive to be the tallest building in Europe but this may happen naturally. One thing is certain: the tower is designed to be a sharp and light presence in the London skyline. Architecture is about telling stories and expressing visions, and memory is part of it. Our memory is permeated by history. That is why this design alludes to spires. One final important point," concludes Renzo Piano, "St Paul's Cathedral is an extraordinary monument and an intrinsic part of London's heritage. I believe that the new tower will not disturb its stateliness. They are breathing the same air, sharing the same atmosphere; they are nurtured at the same source."

Prizes

Life and Work

Renzo Piano was born in September **1937** in Genoa, Italy. He studied in Florence and in Milan, where he worked in the office of Franco Albini and experienced the first student rebellions of the 1960s. Born into a family of builders, frequent visits to his father Carlo's building sites gave him the opportunity to combine practical and academic experience. He graduated from the Politecnico University in Milan in **1964**.

From **1965 to 1970**, he combined his first experimental work with his brother Ermanno together with numerous trips to the UK and the US.

In 1971, he set up the Piano & Rogers office in London with Richard Rogers. Together they won the competition for the Pompidou Center and he subsequently moved to Paris. From the early 1970s to the 1990s, he worked with the engineer Peter Rice, sharing the Atelier Piano & Rice from **1977 to 1981**.

In **1981**, the Renzo Piano Building Workshop (RPBW) was established, and it currently has a staff of 150 and offices in Paris, Genoa, and New York. RPBW has designed buildings all around the world.

Some of his most important current projects include the redevelopment and enlargement of the Harvard Art Museums in Cambridge, the Whitney Museum of American Art and the Campus of Columbia University in New York, the London Bridge Tower, and the Stavros Niarchos Foundation Cultural Center in Athens.

Married to Milly, he lives in Paris and has four children: Carlo, Matteo, Lia, and Giorgio.

Opposite page:
Renzo Piano, 2007
Photograph by Stefano Goldberg

Left:
Renzo Piano in the Resnick Pavilion, 2010
Photograph by Yosi A. R-Pozeilov

Collaborators

1971–77 ▸ Centre Georges Pompidou, Paris, France; *Client*: Ministry of Cultural Affairs, Ministry of National Education; Studio Piano & Rogers, architects

1996–2000 ▸ Refurbishment of the Centre Georges Pompidou, Paris, France; *Client*: Centre Georges Pompidou; Renzo Piano Building Workshop, architects

1982–86 ▸ The Menil Collection, Houston, Texas, USA; *Client*: The Menil Foundation; Piano & Fitzgerald, architects

1985–2001 ▸ Redevelopment of the Old Harbor of Genoa, Genoa, Italy; *Client*: City of Genoa + Porto Antico SpA; Renzo Piano Building Workshop, architects

1983–2003 ▸ Lingotto Factory Conversion, Turin, Italy; *Client*: Fiat S.p.A. (Competition, 1983); *Clients*: Lingotto S.p.A. + Pathé + Palazzo Grassi (Design Development and Construction phase, 1991–2003); Renzo Piano Building Workshop, architects

2000–02 ▸ The Giovanni and Marella Agnelli Art Gallery at Lingotto, Turin, Italy; *Client*: Lingotto S.p.A. + Palazzo Grassi; Renzo Piano Building Workshop, architects

1990–94 ▸ Kansai International Airport Terminal, Osaka, Japan; *Client*: Kansai International Airport Co. Ltd.; Renzo Piano Building Workshop, architects; N. Okabe, senior partner in charge in association with Nikken Sekkei Ltd., Aéroports de Paris, Japan Airport Consultants Inc.

1989–91 ▸ Renzo Piano Building Workshop Punta Nave, Genoa, Italy; *Client*: Renzo Piano Building Workshop; Renzo Piano Building Workshop, architects

1991–2001 ▸ Banca Popolare di Lodi, Lodi, Italy; *Client*: Banca Popolare di Lodi; Renzo Piano Building Workshop, architects

1993–98 ▸ Jean-Marie Tjibaou Cultural Center, Nouméa, New Caledonia; *Client*: Agence pour le Développement de la Culture Kanak; Renzo Piano Building Workshop, architects

1992–2000 ▸ Potsdamer Platz, Berlin, Germany; *Client*: Daimler-Chrysler AG; Renzo Piano Building Workshop, architects; in association with Christoph Kohlbecker (Gaggenau)

1991–97 ▸ Beyeler Foundation Museum, Riehen (Basel), Switzerland; *Client*: Beyeler Foundation; Renzo Piano Building Workshop, architects; in association with Burckhardt + Partner AG, Basel

1997–2001 ▸ Niccolò Paganini Auditorium, Parma, Italy; *Client*: City of Parma; Renzo Piano Building Workshop, architects

1998–2001 ▸ Maison Hermès, Tokyo, Japan; *Client*: Hermès Japon; Renzo Piano Building Workshop, architects; in collaboration with Rena Dumas Architecture Intérieure (Paris)

1994–2002 ▸ Parco della Musica Auditorium, Rome, Italy; *Client*: City of Rome; Renzo Piano Building Workshop, architects

1996–2000 ▸ Aurora Place, office and residential buildings, Sydney, Australia; *Client*: Lend Lease Development; Renzo Piano Building Workshop, architects; in collaboration with Lend Lease Design Group, Sydney (Schematic Design, 1996); in collaboration with Lend Lease Design Group and Group GSA Pty Ltd, Sydney (Design Development and Construction phase, 1997–2000)

1999–2003 ▸ Nasher Sculpture Center, Dallas, Texas, USA; *Client*: The Nasher Foundation; Renzo Piano Building Workshop, architects

1999–2005 ▸ Zentrum Paul Klee, Bern, Switzer-land; *Client*: Maurice E. and Martha Müller Foundation; Renzo Piano Building Workshop, architects; in collaboration with ARB, architects (Bern)

1999–2005 ▸ High Museum of Art Expansion, Atlanta, Georgia, USA; *Client*: High Museum of Art + Woodruff Arts Center; Renzo Piano Building Workshop, architects; in collaboration with Lord, Aeck & Sargent Inc., architects (Atlanta)

2000–06 ▸ Morgan Library Renovation and Expansion, New York, New York, USA; *Client*: The Morgan Library; Renzo Piano Building Workshop, architects; in collaboration with Beyer Blinder Belle LLP (New York)

2000–07 ▸ The New York Times Building, New York, New York, USA; *Client*: The New York Times / Forest City Ratner Companies; Renzo Piano Building Workshop, architects; in colla-boration with FXFowle Architects, P.C. (New York)

2005–08 ▸ California Academy of Sciences Renovation and Expansion, San Francisco, California, USA; *Client*: California Academy of Sciences; Renzo Piano Building Workshop, architects; in collaboration with Stantec Architecture (San Francisco)

2005–09 ▸ Modern Wing of the Art Institute of Chicago, Chicago, Illinois, USA; *Client*: The Art Institute of Chicago; Renzo Piano Building Workshop, architects; in collaboration with Interactive Design Inc., architects (Chicago)

2001–10 ▸ Central Saint Giles Mixed-Use Development, London, UK; *Client*: Legal & General with Mitsubishi Estate Corporation Stanhope PLC; Renzo Piano Building Workshop, architects; in collaboration with Fletcher Priest Architects (London)

2003–08 ▸ Broad Contemporary Art Museum (LACMA Expansion – Phase I), Los Angeles, California, USA; *Client*: Los Angeles County Museum of Art (LACMA); Renzo Piano Building Workshop, architects; in collaboration with Gensler Associates (Santa Monica)

2006–10 ▸ The Resnick Pavilion (LACMA Expansion – Phase II), Los Angeles, California, USA; *Client*: Los Angeles County Museum of Art (LACMA); Renzo Piano Building Workshop, architects; in collaboration with Gensler Associates (Santa Monica)

2004–12 ▸ London Bridge Tower, London, UK; *Client*: Sellar Property Group; Renzo Piano Building Workshop, architects; in collaboration with Adamson Associates (Toronto, London)

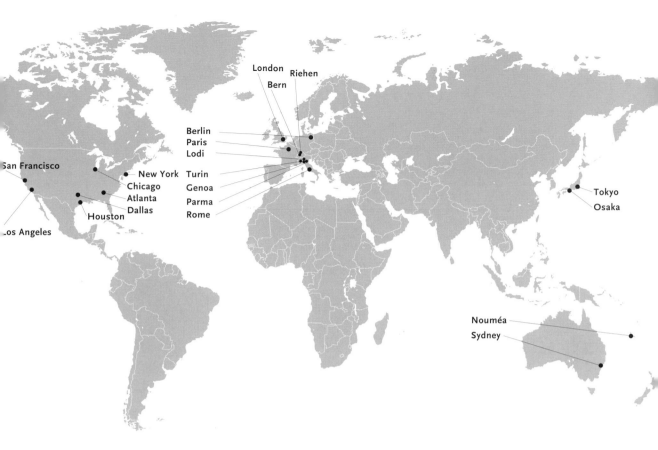

World Map

Bibliography

M. Dini: *Renzo Piano. Progetti e architetture 1964-1983*, Electa, Milan, Italy, 1983

R. Piano: *Progetti e Architetture 1984-1986*, Electa, Milan, Italy, 1986

R. Piano: *Renzo Piano*, Editions du Centre Pompidou, Paris, France, 1987

R. Piano: *Renzo Piano Buildings and Projects 1971-1989*, Rizzoli International, New York, USA, 1989

R. Piano: *Renzo Piano Building Workshop 1964-1991, In Search of a Balance*, Process architecture, Tokyo, Japan, n. 100, 1992

P. Buchanan: *Renzo Piano Building Workshop. Complete Works*, Vol. 1 Phaidon Press, London, UK, 1993

R. Piano: *The Making of Kansai International Airport Terminal*, Kodansha, Tokyo, Japan, 1994

JA n°15: *Kansai International Airport Passenger Terminal Building*, 1994

KIAC: *Construction of the Kansai International Airport Terminal*, KIAC, 1995

P. Buchanan: *Renzo Piano Building Workshop. Complete Works*, Vol. 2, Phaidon Press, London, UK, 1995

R. Piano: *Giornale di bordo*, Passigli ed., Florence, Italy, 1997

K. Frampton: *Renzo Piano Building Workshop*, GA Architect, n° 14, A.D.A. Edita Tokyo, Tokyo, Japan, 1997

P. Buchanan: *Renzo Piano Building Workshop. Complete Works*, Vol. 3, Phaidon Press, London, UK, 1997

P. Buchanan: *Renzo Piano Building Workshop. Complete Works*, Vol. 4, Phaidon Press, London, UK, 2000

R. Piano: *Spirit of Nature – Wood Architecture Award 2000*, Helsinki, Finland, 2000

A. Bensa: *Ethnologie & Architecture-Le centre culturel Tjibaou-une réalisation de Renzo Piano*, Adam Birò, Paris, France, 2000

W. Blaser: *Kulturzentrum der Kanak/ Cultural Centre of the Kanak People*, Birkhäuser, Basel, Switzerland, 2001

A. Metcalf, M. Van der Wal: *Aurora Place-Renzo Piano Sydney*, The Watermark Press, Sydney, Australia, 2001

A. Cuito: *Renzo Piano*, LOFT Publications, Barcelona, Spain, 2002

E. Pizzi: *Renzo Piano*, Birkhäuser, Switzerland, 2002

M. A. Segantini: *Auditorium Parco della Musica*, Federico Motta Editore, Milan, Italy, 2004

R. Piano: *On Tour with Renzo Piano*, Phaidon Press, London, UK, 2004

F. Irace: *Trasparenze e Prospettiva – Renzo Piano a Lodi*; Bolis Edizioni, Bergamo, Italy, 2004

P. Jodidio, PIANO - *Renzo Piano Building Workshop 1966-2005*; Taschen, Cologne, Germany, 2005

R. Piano: *Giornale di bordo*, Passigli ed., Florence, Italy, 2005 – re-edition

R. Cassigoli: *La responsabilità dell'architetto*, Passigli editore, Florence, Italy, 2007 – re-edition

R. Piano, Olivier Favier: *La désobéissance de l'architecte*, Arléa ed., Paris, France, 2007

R. Piano: *Renzo Piano Building Workshop 1990-2006*, AV Monografias (Arquitectura Viva) n° 119, May–June 2006

V. Newhouse: *Renzo Piano Museums*, Monacelli Press, New York, USA, 2007

C. Conforti, F. Dal Co': *Renzo Piano gli schizzi*, Electa, Milan, Italy, 2007

B. Panerai: *Rocca di Frassinello – Una cantina in Maremma secondo Renzo Piano – A Winery in Maremma by Renzo Piano*, Fattoria Editrice, Milan, Italy, 2007

R. Piano The Menil Collection, Monograph, Renzo Piano Foundation, 2007

R. Piano Che cos'è l'architettura? (What Is Architecture?), Luca Sossella ed., Milan, Italy, 2007 (CD and booklet)

R. Piano Fondation Beyeler, Monograph, Renzo Piano Foundation, 2008

P. Jodidio: *PIANO – Renzo Piano Building Work-shop 1966 to Today*, Taschen, Cologne, Germany, 2008

P. Buchanan: *Renzo Piano Building Workshop, Complete Works*, Vol. 5, Phaidon Press, London, UK, 2008

J. Cuno, P. Goldberger, J. Rosa, *The Modern Wing – Renzo Piano and the Art Institute of Chicago*, Yale University Press, Chicago, USA, 2009

R. Piano: *Nouméa Centre Culturel Jean Marie Tjibaou*, Renzo Piano Foundation, 2009

S. Boeri, A. Foppiano, G. Silva: "Being Renzo Piano," *6 mesi in diretta con il mestiere dell'architettura/ 6 Months' Experience of Architecture in the Making*," special edition of the interior design architecture art magazine *Abitare*, no. 497, November 4, 2009

A+U: *Renzo Piano Building Workshop 1989-2010*, Tokyo, 2010

Credits

The Author

Philip Jodidio studied art history and economics at Harvard, and edited *Connaissance des Arts* for over 20 years. His books include TASCHEN's *Architecture Now!* series, and monographs on Tadao Ando, Norman Foster, Richard Meier, Jean Nouvel, and Zaha Hadid. He is internationally renowned as one of the most popular writers on the subject of architecture.